Stephen Debonrepos

New Old Stuff
poems

cover by burpo

nobigfiles@hotmail.com

New Old Stuff,
poems

contents

P.K.F.
Just Waiting For The Check
(I-III)

Four Sonnets
Three Horizons Away

Lady Day (to Billie Holiday)

This is the best
part of the day
the only part
that takes its knee
off my chest

The sun has grumbled off
having finished another
thankless shift
leaving my tiny room
to expand and soften

I sit next to the lamp
that glows a hot apricot
and I stop for a moment
and a half

Secrets
aren't just for people
with something to hide

Secrets are for those
who have people
to hide things from

I have no secrets

I do not need to sneak
in or out
I could come and go
but I mostly
stay

(well... except maybe for groceries)

My fingertips
softly pop
as I turn the cool metal stereo knob
to let you in
Oh, how deeply
do you come in

When I go bonkers
when I go nuts
when I am swinging
off my hinge
I go
I mean, I go far
farther than a wandering boy
on a Saturday

Do I go too far?
Is one star really any
closer to your porch
than any other star?

But, no matter how high I hover
in the freezing wind
no matter how far
into the stars I tumble
no matter how far
I slide onto the spike
no matter how lost
I could possibly get,

I always come back
and only to you
I always come back to you

I love how you wait

'til I've fallen asleep
to gather your things and leave

I don't want to wake my neighbor
so I pitch my voice down low
the whole world is still
but for the graveyard
The moon had somewhere better to go

But I beg you to not speak in whispers
I need the blood that's in your voice
I latch onto the sound like a nipple
It's the closest I come to rejoice

I would not care one bit
if you didn't love me in return
I would always come back
        always come back
        always come back to you

You pour like rifle smoke
out of second-hand speakers
You run your hands
through my tangles
and fill me like a fire hose

You creak and you sway
and I'm almost okay

Okay, that is
until you leave
and you must always leave

You leave when
my head is an orange
that was used to make juice

and now has nowhere to go
but an unlaundered pillow

I don't know why
and I'll never ask
never ask the sun
what exactly happened
between the two of you

The River

I now only see it in snatches
while driving along River Road
while winding through the
cyclists and redwoods,
while sifting through static and code

It bulges when full of its tourist canoes
or after a season of rain
It's creeks are reduced to a trickle
when drought is collapsing its veins

The summers when I was more human
I used to go up to my chin
Those days of guitars and sack lunches
back then, when to play was to win

I am now upholstered with blubber
My hipbone, it creaks and it hurts
I hobble around like a toddler
and my decency comes out in spurts

The river would never refuse me
nor does it await my return
no magnetic field surrounds it
I am no point of concern

I live half a block from the river
my knees think I live on the dunes
I still say that I love of the river
the way that I know that it's noon

Fine Time

Some of the finest time
that one can spend
is found within a room that has a TV
and this TV
is turned off.
Its glow dies like a ghost
having delivered its message
and there's that unsettling feeling
a jet lag of sorts
arrival into a tilted land
where one travels on foot
and time is measured
by looking into the sky.

It is you,
and alone, you inflate the room
pushing out every rubbery corner
with your temperament,
your true temperament
(well, another true temperament)
your secret humour,
the richness of flavor
found in one's own company,
before you turn the TV back on

Finally Bring You Back

I want to sing a song
that would kill Roberta Flack
make the Pope take up the drums
and finally bring you back

I want to push some paint around

to swirl it, stare and whack
to make the critics waiters
and to finally bring you back

I want to scrawl out words
that'll make TVs go black
to make the scholars lovesick
and to finally bring you back

It's youth and notoriety
not romance that I lack
no matter what I try, I know
I'll never get you back

What Kind?

What kind of neighbor am I?
What kind of neighbor am I?
I'm screening your calls
through these rice paper walls
What kind of neighbor am I?

What kind of dancer am I?
What kind of dancer am I?
learned to waltz and to stroll
just to hump on a pole
What kind of dancer am I?

What kind of lover am I?
What kind of lover am I?
to corral and seduce
then say you're of no use
What kind of lover am I?

What kind of creature am I?
What kind of creature am I?
a unicorn parked at the door of the ark
What kind of creature am I?

What kind of scribbler am I?
What kind of scribbler am I?
giving birth to these critters
not by one, but in litters
What kind of scribbler am I?

What kind of writer am I?
What kind of writer am I?
making puns in a tongue
that's now spoken by none
What kind of writer am I?

E.C.

Whenever you cross my mind
I make a fist
I always make a fist
'cause you always cross my mind

A Poem about J.C. Leyendecker

We won World War II
but we might not have
had you stayed over there
stayed in Germany
and not stood in line
with all of the others
in 1882

The posters!
The posters!
The covers of all those magazines!
They were all the proof
one would ever need,
ever need for anything!

It was in
The Saturday Evening Post
that you gave birth
to The New Year's Baby
the one who'd grow up to
slick down his hair
and wear only
Arrow Shirt collars
and receive marriage proposals
by the sackload

But look at the strokes
Just look at those strokes!
Your strokes, they were mad
in their confidence
and yet, had the restraint
of a retiring judge

Your strokes showed me

showed us all
how the fringe on a tabletop lamp
was as sexy as a
seasoned fan dancer

The sleeve on a collegiate blazer
might as well be a stained glass window
and a circle of Winter trees
an Easter cathedral

You showed Mussolini about
Style and Power
You showed Uncle Sam
how an orphan can love

But now,
you are merely a footnote
a footnote on the biographies
of lesser men

Once you were flesh
a blood-filled sponge
with a sister and two brothers
oceans apart from one another
Francis, living in your shadow
and Mary, dying in her own

But, you also had your live-in lover,
handsome Charles Beach,
strapping Charles Beach
the sight of whom
changed one's breathing

He was a muse
but that didn't excuse him

from acting like family
and we all know how family acts

There was also Norman
Norman at your hem
Norman who couldn't see
what you saw in men

Young Rockwell worshipped
and hated you, as well
for splitting his young boy's mind
into halves that never could re-weld

Like so many who'd come
across on the ferry
you thought that you'd never stop

never stop working
never stop earning
never stop taking
every single commission
never stop hiring
the finest of models
never stop always
arriving in limos
never stop spending
never stop wearing
suits and tuxedoes
even while painting
never stop holding
a brush without shaking
never stop signing
your name without squinting

It would go on and on forever...

But, everybody dies
and before that, we grow old
Our strength leaves our bodies
to crash better parties

Your body, a handful
of pieces of chalk
was now rattling around
in a shirt and some slacks

and now, gone was your brother
and gone was the other
and what's left your sister
was not worth the bother

Gone was your day
Over, your Summer

Just a Jeopardy! answer
that ends with the buzzer

Now, you are nothing
nothing but my favorite
but as any gravedigger knows
that's only
a matter of time

Bedquilt- *Aroma Roasters, Santa Rosa, CA 2001*

From how far away
do they come?
these sweatshirted couples,
the cubicle refugees,
to these lush rolling vineyards
each weekend?

According to Dorothy Parker,
Sonoma goes easily
toe to toe
with any two-thousand Bordeaux

I sit at the window
with my jittery stare
pure puppy eagerness
sipping 'til tipping
my ears of no use

Nursing my coffee
I try to still myself
to encourage the soak
that impatience impedes

Sonoma
it is your women
that take the blue ribbons
Tie them to hats of street market straw
Let them fly from ponytails
and coaster brake Huffys

Pump your vines hard
and suck from beneath,
soil brownie moist and a thousand miles deep

to ripen your women
engorged with the juices of sleep

The Rabbi Said

The rabbi said "You would make a good Jew"
I said "I don't think there's a God"
"Details," he said without moving his head
and I felt a compulsion to nod

All Of My Songs Sound The Same

I bought a guitar at the swap meet
would fin'lly get into the game
My mother came home
and she smashed it to bits
Now all of my songs sound the same

I got a guitar from my grandpa
and wanted to cause him no shame
but I knew no rancheros and only three chords
and now all of my songs sound the same

I brought my guitar to the party
and banged it to drunken acclaim
Why would I trade what had gotten me laid?
Now, all of my songs sound the same

I wrecked my guitar in a car crash
I'm lucky I wasn't struck lame
The settlement covered the doctor
... just barely
Now all of my songs sound the same

Another one brought me the treasures
that vanished as fast as they came
They now are just stains
on the walls of my brain
and all of my songs sound the same

I hocked my guitar for mere pennies,
so I wouldn't be out in the rain
I knew there's no way it would ever forgive me
Now all of my songs sound the same

A new guitar stands in the corner,

projecting accusal and blame
Mundane-ing, migraining
I'm always complaining
and all of my songs sound the same

My guitar and I have an arrangement
I haven't the juice to explain
The wish I hold dear
is to just disappear
and all of my songs sound the same

Christmas Poem

Impossibly black
Impossibly clean
The icy December sky
is sprayed with stars that sparkle
as if scrubbed entirely new

As the Jack o' Lanterns
begin to soften and smell
on November porches
I pack away my bah humbug
as most folks are dragging out
boxes of tangled lights
and salt and flour ornaments

This is the time
for egg nog and pumpkin pie milkshakes
at Jack in the Box,
for six hundred versions of Silent Night
played on the local radio station
between late-night dedications
phone calls from ghosts
disembodied voices begging forgiveness
and pleas for donations of
coats for the poor
This and watching Charlie Brown cartoons
for the forty-third time

It's time for playing my
Yamaha digital piano
for my rather preoccupied cat

This is not God's time
For God's time is always
and time's a big nothing

No, this is a time for the lights
lights of red
lights that throb
lights that flash
lights that don't

It's time for the trees
we bring inside
whose piny smell
shoots up my nose
and tousles my hair

The family tensions I hear so much of
pass me by and over my head
like a twister, pulling whole trees
by their roots
tossing tractors and trucks
across the gray runny clouds
as I lay low in my cellar
an orphan? deserter?
In a mass grave
I have buried the living
I have escaped by walking the plank
and now I stand straight
as you poor suckers
you dodge the missives
of visiting relatives
the booby-trapped anecdotes
and barbs over dinner

Free Lunch

Slide your tray along
Sometimes you point
Sometimes you say "thank you"
but not much else
Sometimes there's a choice
Today, it's the hot dog or grilled cheese
and a little box of milk
A square slab of peanut butter
dusted with powdered sugar
makes for a mid-day dessert
(Dessert? at lunch?
At home, we don't usually get it with dinner!)
After a while

you stop giving your name
The register lady knows who's on the list
The cafeteria's a budget cathedral
Nobody cared
who got free lunch
Maybe the parents
but nobody else
Not until now, anyway

All I Want to Do is Cry

She asked me to a movie
I didn't want to lie
I told her I can't make it
All I want to do is cry

I should do the laundry
I should straighten up this sty
I should get some perspective
All I want to do is cry

I should finally knock it off
give it another try
I should return your calls but
all I want to do is cry

Let it out or keep it in
I should fin'lly break the tie
Confession heals the soul but
all I want to do is cry

I cannot seem to move an inch
I cannot answer why
and if I knew, why'd I tell you?
All I want to do is cry

There's too much goddamn light in here
My veins are going dry
That's not what I call music
All I want to do is cry

It'll prob'ly end like this
no more to sell nor buy
It's about time that I left
All I want to do is cry

Monte Rio, in February

Through the rain-blackened redwoods
a shaft of sun, thick as a butter stick
is turning my drooling window
into steam

Talking to You

No, it's no trouble
and no I don't mind
Tell me all your problems
and I'll spare you mine

I enjoy talking to you
We always say
the same things

I don't enjoy talking to them
They always say
the same things

You Take Your Time

You are my hero
You are a man
a man
who takes his time

My cat is off
crouching somewhere
I'm grateful
for your slow, sad music
and this low, soft light
at 3am

You take your time
like the wobbly old man
at the supermarket
who slowly
cuts in front of you
in the checkout line

Give Myself to You

All that I could give
I've given
All that I could risk
I've lost
All I have of my old love
are crumbs
crumbs amongst all of the dust

Now, I really need to give
and as long as I'm to live

All I want to do
is give myself to you
All I want to do
is give myself to you

For me, it's all or nothing
and nothing in-between
wherever it may take me
what it may or may not mean
All I want to do
is give myself to you

What I've got is old and worn
wasn't much when it was new
but I'll shine it up the best I can
and give it all to you

I want to give myself to you
the only promise mine
I ask nothing in return
I don't expect a sign

All I want to do

is give myself to you...

I have nothing you could possibly want
but I am on my knees, I need
to give myself to you

Holiday

Not another holiday
Not another day of
Americans observing nothing
nothing but the desire not to go to work
of bank doors that say "no"

Not another day of full-page ads
and prices slashed
for sixteen hours only

There is only one reason left
for the closing off of streets
for marching bands
and hot dog stands

Only one reason
to stand at the blackboard
and tell the class
to put their workbooks away

Only one reason
to gather in circles
holding hands
with our chins to our chests
and that reason
is your face

God and I

My first introduction to God was at
the table where donuts were set
I extended my hand and told me, coldly
that we had already met

I called out to God in the evening
not certain that he would pick up
He did and kept asking "Who is this?"
so much I could not interrupt

I thought I saw God in a bookstore
The cops, they had him by the wrist
I thought I saw God in a bookstore
but bookstores no longer exist

Far From Home

Home, as it lives in my head
is a pink stucco box in Covina
it's nineteen seventy-four
Stray cats come through the open window
the sun is like orange juice with pulp
The radio plastic is magic
and I have the place to myself
Ivy cascades o'er the high chain link fence
Avocados, they blacken and swell
The TV is on
only sometimes
and to do is to do something well

Now, I am much bigger
I live in a box

that is tiny
for I live alone
I do not stray far
I mostly stay in
in this box
that is not quite a home

Eight Haiku

Storm clouds moan gently
just like cellos with dry throats
rusting my tin ears

My grey and white cat
wants to poop in the litter
but I got here first

Raindrops make circles
just like the Olympic rings
in a cold puddle

The redwoods are topped
with spikes, black against the grey
I can't risk the climb

Stormy skies above
electricity feeds me
like photography

The sun burns slowly
through a canopy of smog
on my vacation

The Great Lake Eerie
when viewed from the shoreline, just
may be an ocean

Leaves crunch like bacon
beneath my Converse All Stars
too late for breakfast

I Know Nothing

I know nothing
about these plasticky pills
but take 'em, I do
You bet'cha

I know nothing
of any nearness to God
but my fingertips meet
by the moon

I know nothing
of love, but know that I broke
your heart
trying to figure it out

Yes, I know nothing
but I am not likely
to ever be
shutting up soon

I am an expert on nothing
an expert on nothing
on nothing
and nothing at all

I know nothing
of four different kinds of friendship
and it's always too late when I call

I know nothing
but all of the time that I've wasted
the things I have chas-ed
down so many promising holes

I know nothing
after all the near-deathly trips
upon sinking ships

I remember, of course
those days,
memories that expand
like sponge capsule animals
memories of buttery kisses
and sleeping outside
in the Summertime
Days of uncherished glory
Days of sloppy euphoria

I could go on a quiz show
my mortarboard
topping my head full of nothing
nothing but noise
all noise and nothing

nothing but how now
it always is squeezing,
It's squeezing and so very hard

I know nothing
I am the Shakespeare of Clever Excuses
The Mozart of Amateur Pain

I have the syntax
and the grammar
I make my case
without a stammer
and without knowing much
of anything

You Are Alone

You are alone
God has left
and didn't say
when he'd be back

I Talk to God in the Darkness

I do not always call it poetry
true, that it's rhyming in verse
but to my disdain, all I do is complain
and it's seeming to only get worse

I talk to god in the darkness
I talk to god in the silence
I talk to god in the absence
I talk to god in-between

I have no art
that hangs on my walls
no music
that hangs in the air
there's no more dancing
left in these legs
I have no poetry
to cobble and scrawl
just a list
of groceries
to buy

I talk to god in the darkness
I talk to god in the silence
I talk to god in the absence
I talk to god in-between

I do not always call it poetry
true, that it's rhyming in verse
but to my disdain, all I do is complain
and it's seeming to only get worse

Awful

I awoke to a loose pile of tiny grey feathers
where I really should put an area rug

I'd really hoped you'd made it out

That day, you came in, swooping and crashing
like a act in a carnival tent

As much as a man my size can
I tried to chase you out and away
to shoo you through the door
or out the window through which you had come
as my cat watched intently
like a juiced referee

My place is so tiny
but with plenty of places
a bluebird who's lost could go hide
After a while, you'd just disappeared
and I didn't know if you're still inside

I worried and fretted,
called friends who, "I bet" -ted
I left out some bread in a bowl

I hoped and I prayed
that you hadn't stayed
that you'd escaped
because such was the goal

but this morning my bladder
poked as it does

every half hour or so
and I found the soft splatter
of your tiny feathers
before I saw you on the floor

Your tiny body
still blue but now stiff
made me flinch as I sought
napkins for covering it

How long did it take you to die?
I tried to count up the days
the days since you look that Hitchcockian left
and watched most of your choices fly 'way

A slow death it was,
not outside in the Winter,
the cold that broke records this year
No, you quietly lay, awake, scared and starving
while my cat and I watched reruns on Fox
before wishing "Sweet dreams" to each other

You had a horrible death
You died on Christmas Eve
and plumbers charge triple on the day before Christmas
so my miniature victim, my medieval guest
I'll not try the toilet
but place you in the trash
amongst all of the boxes that had previously brought in
all of those frozen dinners

Where is it?

Where is my jar of honey?
It's gone and I've looked everywhere
I need something sunny to put in my tummy
or I'm an unfortunate bear

Where is my ukelele?
I'm feeling the needing to sing
I do this daily, so come home Bill Bailey
or else my step has no spring

Where is my purple yo-yo?
It was in my pocket, right here
I need it to swing, though a cradle of string
as yo-yo season draws near

Where is my pirate kitty?
The one with the patch on his eye
I think he's good luck, but he owes me four bucks
so I don't think that he's coming by

Where is my favorite kite?
I think it might be up a tree
I flew it last week, hit a crow in the beak
so that crow has a thing against me

You Can Do This

You can do this
I tell the mirror
the way your mother
tells you you're pretty
the way a teacher

will say there's still time
still time to pull up those grades

You can do this
I say like a girl
who wants to "stay friends"
like a doctor who says
"That depends"

I say it again
You can do this
You can do this

Let Me Be Loving

Let me be loving
and let me do right
let me not buckle
when I'm supposed to fight

Let me not bicker
with those who need love
Let me be not below
nor be not above
Let me be loving
and be only love

I want to love everyone
to say it and really to mean it
to be able to really say something
and when I do this
to feel it

to have an opinion on nothing
to really let everything go
and to not feel the bursting need
to let everybody know

to want what I've got
and eat just enough
to give, not expecting a thing
to walk unaffected by the staring
that walking past strangers will bring

to tell the whole truth without
hurting a soul
to not get on anyone's nerves
to be famous only for keeping my word
to give more than I think I deserve

to no longer fly off the handle
to let all the little things slide
and to see that some big stuff is little
when viewed from a different side

to do all the things I'm supposed to
despite all my body's complaints
to pray like I wasn't a skeptic
like I hadn't offended the saints

to not want to break people in anger
to not want in a rage to throw things
to not dwell as much upon what I might need
as what I could possibly bring

seeing my fellow without looking down
without looking up or away
truly seeing him as my equal
and loving us both anyway

My Old Self

The doctor says
it's a sign of improvement
that it means
that I'm growing stronger

I finally have, he says
the strength
the strength to be angry
the strength I would need
to bankroll some rage
the strength to blame God
for this spiked anatomical cage

When I was feeble
and could not lift my head
I was like Jesus
I'd made The Deal
looking the Universe
square in the eye

I floated
not above
but somewhere
somewhere else
not like a rising balloon
but like a jellyfish
who just can't decide

I felt only love
for each
and for all

Never again
would I stand

Not like that

Never again
would I take a position
against another

This disease
a disease of dirty blood
had peeled me completely
and my pulp was dispersing like gas

The pain
the mind-ripping pain
had truly boiled me clean
like a scalpel
making noisy toys of the medical machines
turning words into things
that kids used to fish out of soup

I was held in place by a hospital bed
I was a skirt around Saturn
I was woozy and wise
I was asking the nurse
for the sunscreen
endorsed by Joan of Arc

But now I am feeling much better
I'm re-emerging from shock
Now I return to the bacon skin
that wraps me like swaddling cloth

Now, strength fills my limbs
like fire hoses
I'm returning to anger
to judgement
to smallness
to my old self

I gave myself completely
to the footprint of a cloud
shot myself into the heart of Zero
started down the curling path
of the question mark
I bowed to the molecules
blocked by the sun

Orphans

I've done the laundry
The dishes are done
and she's as safe
as one gets in a hospital

So, now I'm back home
on the sofa
just a long-winded bore
alone with his medieval head
a piece, trying to pry himself
away from the rest of the puzzle

Is it really a fight?
Is it really a struggle
or just wriggling?
When you are shaking,
what are you shaking against?
Are you shaking against anything?
Is there such a thing
as a valiant vibration?
Is there something to defeat
or to win?

When hysterical limbs
try to rid themselves
of their bones
due to pills for the noise
that just... will... not...
stop.

After all of the flailing
the wailing and failing,
the repeated impaling
is there ever a victor?

A winner, a road block parade?
or is there only
wave after wave
of orphans in rubble
orphans awoken
each morning
by sirens

Sunday Outing

In another forty-five minutes
I will go back to my room
my time in the yard will be over
the warden's routine will resume

In another thirty-five minutes
I'll put on my hat and I'll go
I'll slide my hand
'long the cool of the railing
and descend to the cellars below

In another twenty-five minutes
my time on the clock will be up
I will slither away
and have nothing to say
though nothing I say would disrupt

In another ten and five minutes
my permit is set to expire
The dancers will all continue to dance,
the spark plugs continue to fire

In only another five minutes
the big door behind me will close
and my afternoon out
will be merely about
a mannequin shifting its pose

The Rot Behind My Eyes

The rot behind my eyes
it is bulging
The wobble in my walk
it is back
The heat that's in my haircut
sets fire
to ears of quickly cascading wax

it leaves my mouth a hinge
that is broken
I can't see through all of the goo
cannot make a dent in the membrane

All of this is through the hiss
There's still so much to do
ever so much
to do

and it'll never ever happen
not all of it get done

not like this, through all the hiss

best get to it
best get back
right back to square one

But A Ghost

Things are getting better.
They are almost going good,
but herein lies the danger.
What I do's not what I should

Surely now I can afford
to miss a dose or two,
relax my grip
as tires slip across the line I drew.

Things are going better.
I've been sleeping through the night.
My fingers do night drop the pen
nor grip it 'til they're white.

I'm not heady, even giddy.
I for now don't have to beg.
Hardly notice how I swagger
as I drag my wooden leg.

Things are going better
and my voice goes up a notch,
as everyone's performance
goes reported on my watch.

I've got something in my pocket
and so tighter is my fist
and everyone's a suspect
and goes on the suspect list.

Things are going better
so my head is full of foam.
Since this isn't my hometown
I do as they in Rome.

Diet Coke is my champagne.
The bar's without a host.
I was certainly a better man
when I was but a ghost.

Too Late for Magic

Of course,
I thought
it is too late
in this life of mine
for magic

Then the phone rang
and it was you

Of course
I could be there
lickety-split
You could catch
your death of rain and cold

Stopped at a red light
you kissed me, twice
and the sky pulled back
its grey curtain
as if the rain
had washed the stars clean
and arranged us a private display

You invited me in
and kissed me again
I tucked each kiss
in my pocket

Thinking that each one
might be the last
I did nothing at all
to stop it

I'd known you by day

and would so again
but tonight,
tonight there was magic
and you never want magic to end

Unit *-For Aren*

Travel it well with little to carry
a world that will never be yours
and realize, halfway around
that it is your only home

There is nothing sturdy enough
against which to crash your bones
No shatter
No new shape

When I first met your throbbing addict's stare
your mouth of razors and foam
you drew me through your nostrils deep

Now I write to you sister,
amputee,
butcher's map,
with a stolen pen

It spits and spins out a frizzled mess
spoiling the promise
of the perfectly white
and empty page
until casual observers draw a rectangle around it
and hang it above a fireplace
that runs on gas

If there is evil in nature
We are guilty in word
and trapped in deed

They may spot you
they may gather 'round
and say we can fix you

Slice here
Chop there
Its ends will grow over
with skin

Yellow '57 Chevy

Whether plodding by foot
or flying by bike
I would pass the long yellow Chevy
on my way To
or on my way From
for what surely must've been years

Banged into being in late fifty-six
it was Space Age fins
hammered onto a hearse
a radio with wings!
It was the one and only reason
you wanted to ever grow up

Its mirrors were decoration only
There was only punching the gas
and no looking back
I wanted it
I ached for it
I pined and whimpered for it

If it were mine
I wouldn't name it, no sir
Some people name their cars
but naming your stuff
was for losers
or old guys with beards who play Jazz

If it were mine
all the friends
I had kept in my head
would pile into it
like the Monkees

and I would captain us
right to the beach
bouncing along the road
like a loud cartoon
Some of my friends
would be girls

That was all I saw
and I saw it each time
each time that I looked
and boy did I look
look at that yellow '57 Chevy

until a sign reading "For Sale"
appeared in it's window
on one morning that kicked off
a fiery day
a day as big as Summer
a day that make the sky bulge
My heart did paradiddles, then just fell
It fell
so far and so long
I didn't know that it ever would land
It was swallowed by darkness
It was swallowed by silence
by a well full of stories of neighborhood accidents
stories all never confirmed
by a well that made boys dog-dare each other
by a well from which nothing returned
I then felt a pain
felt a pain, a very sharp pain
in my empty, empty, empty
fifteen year-old cordoroy pockets

For a coupl'a weeks after
I rode past my love, my crushing love

on my black Huffy cruiser
frantic for a miracle
as my ribs went the way
of a styrofoam cup
and before long
both sign and Chevy were gone

Your Face

Your face
all pink and impossible
makes my face
a busted padlock
hanging by its hook

It leaves me breathing
through my mouth
makes me a photo
of an ape

Am I
of absolutely no use to you?
No,
I'm of no use
to you
at all

Your face
caused a wave of mass firings
Your face
shut the factory down
Your face
killed the new legislation
Your face
changed what they're teaching in school
Your face
was the end of it all
and the end of it all
was your face

Next to most
I am a joke
Next to you

I am an outdoor puff
of cigarette smoke
an odor, dispersing
then forgotten

I know that you could never need me
that you won't remember that we ever met

Your face
undoes all those years of college
Your face
says I'm in the wrong line
Your face
is my mid-term, corrected
Your face
makes the young just give up
Your face
turns us all into statues
Your face
makes a cry in our ribs
Your face
tells us we can stop waiting
Your face
says there's much to forgive

The Bear and the Butterfly

It was all over.
The Bear was in love
the first time that he saw the Butterfly.

He followed her out
of the woods to a clearing
where the wildflowers swayed with the tides.

She closed and expanded
descended and landed
on the tip of the nose of the Bear.

He fumbled his paws
burst into applause
as the Butterfly took to the air.

The Summer suspended
in sunlight and honey,
the Amber that traps and preserves,

this pair of two jumping,
cartwheeling and thumping,
as happy as any deserve.

The sun grew so full
of its nectary burden
that it started to finally drop

and anyone there
would see, and quite clearly,
that this day, like all days, would stop.

If there is a night
then that is alright

for the sun's where the moon
gets its light.

Sleep, Come

Sleep,
Please come
Sleep,
The TV is scraping
the brown from my eyes
and the room, it tilts like a ship
like a ship in a film with an all-star cast

I've been two times down
my head in the pillow
a bowling ball spastically polishing itself
spinning this way then that
like a child on the wrong meds
a child who has worn you down
to the point that all that you feel
when you see him
is the very, very worst

Sleep, come... please come
My only other thought is to eat
I'm weak and I smell
I'm going through Hell
only to wind up back here

My thumb
it stamps and it mashes
it mashes the rubbery buttons
that change what the TV throws back at me

I have to strain to hear what they're saying
for the man with whom I share
a paper-thin wall
is someone I truly, truly
hate

I do not remember
what was just on the screen
the instant I mash it away

Sleep, sleep
I lay myself out like a plate of stale cookies
ones that you buy at the dollar store
ones that are meant to be almost as good
ones that make some children cry

Sleep, sleep, I offer myself
You could be both Santa and gift
You could be an angel
and grant me the wish

to mercifully set me adrift
like heavenly morphine
a buttery, bosomy snowstorm
that seizes my head like a basketball pass
and refuses to ever let go

Sleep, come
I beg of you
the sun is rubbing its hands
It soon will step up
and unzip it's fly
and break us to all it demands

Friday

I am complaining
I'm bitching and moaning
I'm hating and fuming
I'm steaming and raging
I'm pointing the finger
I'm "I told you so"ing
I'm "Poor me, boo-hoo"ing
I'm missing the Old Days
I'm eating in anger
I'm old and I'm tired
I'm sick and I'm aching
and I'm drifting farther and farther
from God

I'm filling up pages
I'm hoping for more
I'm willing to settle
I'm finding it tough
I'm nervous and shaky
I'm stuck and I'm sinking
I'm weary and tired
I'm making corned beef
I'm not sure I'm lonely
I'm waiting and waiting
I'm waiting for nothing
I'm tired of listening
I'm tired of hearing
I'm ready to leave

I Fell In Love With Your Face

I fell in love with your face
Some say this cannot be done

These people are not to be trusted
for love is something even geniuses
have not pinned down

She Says It Comes From Somewhere

Sometimes you ask to know my thoughts
just to tell me that you hate them
Sometimes you hate me for having them

As if I were their author
As if they didn't come to me
like rainstorms

I think back to someone else
another Someone
Who is No Longer Here

She says it comes from somewhere
It must fulfill a need
She says it comes from somewhere
comes from somewhere

She says it tells you something
but, like I said
she's no longer here

So, what are we to do?
What am I to do with you?
What do I do with that
that which you're constantly giving me?
Now, what do I do with that?

You ask me why I'm like this
why I'm doing this to you

Some things cannot be explained
others not explained away
We give each other kisses
We give each other hell

for things that we can neither choose
nor change

The Party Is Raging

The party is raging
with mannequin staging
but I am ready to go

The guests aren't guests
but they're doing their best
and I am ready to go

The women are brothers
high-fiving each other
and I am ready to go

They're calling it music
but they just abuse it
and I am ready to go

Her tongue growing thicker
she wants it all quicker
and I am ready to go

The film machine clacks
like a 'coaster on tracks
and I am ready to go

They're all staring back
'cause I ate all the snacks
and I am ready to go

I showed up too early
far overdressed, surely
and I am ready to go

I'm due before lockdown
The bus don't go downtown

but I am still ready to go

Again Making Lists

Again making lists
of the things that I miss,
the view from a rooftop
that's dy'ng in the sun,
its dirty glow rimming the curving of earth
pockmarked by swimming pools
grubby with shrubs,
a wafer of thin dirty clay,
broken brown eggshell
an area code,
the sun dragging color away.

The moon had told no one
its plans, either way
as the yellowing Hollywood sign
stood like the teeth
of the world's oldest smoker
still smiling at Sunset and Vine.

I long for the lava
that covered the sky
on the tail of that mis'rable day.
I'd wound up on that fiery
rooftop by Chance,
if there is such a thing.
(Who can say?)

A parking garage, hiding just off of La Brea
next to the Bally's that was,
still teeming with amateur cutthroats at mirrors,
in a town where you to pay just to
stop.

I stood at the railing,

while pulling and failing
to take in enough thin air to fill
these crackling lungs, made of paper maché,
next to Time, which had also stood still.

It had been a day long, without any direction,
of nametags on sociopaths
of rolling around like a BB on cardboard,
missing each hole as I pass.

For buckets of days,
I'd been trying to crawl back
onto the calendar's grid,
but the harder I clutched,
the more that I scrambled,
the quicker and farther I slid.

I had a phone in my pocket.
A real one. It wasn't a toy!
Was this the world
that I had imagined,
the future I'd dreamt as a boy?
Was this a world of rockets and robots,
of fireplace girlfriends and Love,
scenarios painted by songs on the radio
the sort we no longer speak of.

Free and unwanted and
blurred and askew
and sliding right off of the Earth
with its slow shifting plates
on such awful a day
such a lifetime away from my birth,

a miserable day, an Agony Best
but within it, I witnessed a crack,

that gave it a mark announcing Act II
and splitting it roughly in half
back when I still had some hydraulic muscle
in what are now legs made of sand
before I was sewn in to this chicken skin
too thin to not wince at the wind.

I am a sore that does not seem to heal
an off remark misunderstood.
How could I know that one day I would say,
Man, did I have it and good.

For B, Upon Her Diagnosis

Our minds, they go
to so many places
places we'd never predict
and then they just go

We wander and tumble
through stars and through brush
We sing and we mumble
We crawl and we rush

I know none of your many mysteries
but I know of them
and I'm glad to have met you
I love and salute you
I reach out to touch you
and I want so much to
draw broadsword to knight you
so shining a knight
that all dragons might flee
just flap into blackness
as you tumble
tumble through the stars

A Poem That Is Not About A Woman

My tongue
it is useless
a spring made of yarn

I love you
These three words
creep past my sleeping tongue
a fat sheriff napping on the porch
of a low budget movie

These three words mean nothing
not from the likes of me
floating a million miles from any planet
hurling pennies at the heart of the sun

I hate you
three words that slip out
like farts during sit ups
three words spat out
automatically like a vending machine
spastic with Tourette's
when a butter knife goes crashing,
and clangs on the floor

I do not defend this
not at all
Just straight reporting
I hate you just feels right
at the moment
that white hot flash
to a man
a man who will never seem to wriggle free
from the strangle and suffocation
of this particular skin

A Man Who Plans To End His Life

A man who plans to end his life
does not deal from beneath
He still will pay his rent on time
He still will brush his teeth

A man who cannot move his arms
nor push through all the tar
cannot make plans to end his life
can't think ahead that far

A man who plans to end his life
may smile at the TV
his eyes not quite as glossy
as they once used to be

A man who plans to end his life
leaves nothing unconfessed
A man who plans to end his life
will always do his best

Motive

Putting words
down on paper
Words
putting down

A Better Lie

Do... Do I dare
push against the dust and pollen
that surrounds me?
Do... Do I dare
push this pen into the tooth of this pad?
Do I dare
inhale what surely must be
too deeply?

Do I dare
sing the song
that brings down
the avalanche?

Is it the Heimlich or clearing one's own throat
Isn't every one entitled to a vote?

Some ears
serve to tell themselves they're wrong
Some ears
serve to tell themselves they're right
Some are
just to hold up glasses
meant to block out all the light

You are what you are
You do what you must
You make do
with whatever you scrape up

So, won't you try, try, try
talking yourself into
a better lie

P.K.F

You've been dead
for nearly a year
and I'm just now writing you this.
I never intended to do so
but, now that I have started
it seems so very, very
late.

Just Waiting For The Check

Pack me in a box of pills
Tape the flaps down tight
There's no need for postage
There is no address to write

This skull is stuffed with bubble wrap
and mucus lines its walls
It's dented from its dealings with
who won't return my calls

Not a box for opening
it's guarding no surprise
Just lower it into the earth
so I may rest my eyes

Just Waiting For The Check, II

No matter how I look around
It seems the waitress can't be found
From the decor, it should be clear
it's not its charm that keeps me here
The meal is done. It wasn't great.
There's still a crime scene on my plate.
I flag a different gal this time
She says, "That station isn't mine."
The radio is stuck between
the nursery rhyme and the obscene
Not that I've somewhere to be,
I'd cut the culprit at the knee
for trapping me within this hive
where flinching is to be alive.
The dishes crash somewhere in back.
These strangers' eyes are an attack.
I try the busboy, wave my hand,

speak slowly so they understand.
I am still Crusoe, freshly wrecked
and I'm still waiting for the check.

Check, Please (Just Waiting For The Check, III)

I'll be glad when this whole thing is over
I am ready to bid a goodbye
to the grunts and the grunting
the hunts and the hunting
the painful charade
of the road-block parades
the dust and the dusting
the busted and busting
the trust and distrusting
the must and the musting
(The Mustang, I like
but I'd swap for a bike
for these hips make the bathroom
an Everest hike)

I won't say goodbye
not the way you think
No one cares 'bout what I might regret
I have dusted your eye
like a piece of junk mail
not important enough to forget

Sonnet #1

She has the skin that's never seen the sun
It cannot keep the secret of her veins
She's every guilty wish, rolled into one
Whomever's choking does not hold the reins

The sight of her disrobed is proof enough
that there is more we have to fear than God
Whatever engineers this kind of stuff
would spoil the Earth to spare the lightning rod

She is the flesh that rumbles into life
She makes the true believer doubt his stance
and as they see the Devil take a wife
the angels wish for just another chance

The anvil-chested blacksmith and the waif,
now that she has awakened, none are safe

Sonnet #2

If Winston Smith can do it, so can I
I'll tunnel out of this and get away
I won't last long on what the pills supply
as I am dragged into another day

I have no faith in that but what I've seen
and that would have to be described as bleak
and most of what exists lie in-between
the ruler notches marking words we speak

I furiously scribble, even though
I only can expect more of the same
I take all the advice that you can throw
so lack of trying can't be ever blamed

The desert sand will scrape and sear your gut
as you crawl on, your eyes cemented shut

Sonnet #3

A wish is but a snapshot of your need
Let's not continue such a childish myth
that heart and head are similarly keyed
and that the bloody muscle weeps herewith

The New Age smart-ass always cracking wise
They claim they to guard the wall 'tween math and art,
the tourists who would come to colonize
but let's not put these whores before Decartes

Upon advice from whom I'd call a friend
I'm trying to imagine what would be
a life that I'd be not so quick to end
a plot development I'd like to see

I don't resist suggestions as they come
but don't tell me that what I feel's not numb

To Keep One Waiting (Sonnet #4)

To keep one waiting is a kind of sin
some kind of lie. It is a sort of theft,
a slap, a double-fuck you wrapped within
a "You Are Not Important. You're What's Left."

You are a "Whoops." You are an "I forgot,"
an "I don't give a shit," "What's it to me?"
"It slipped my mind," and thus, you matter not
You are the "He'll come back, just wait and see."

It bothers some, some others not at all
Some live without detecting it exists
oblivious to standards, as they fall
Some giggle, while the others chew their wrists

A dose of your own medicine would fit
but I don't think that you would notice it.

Three Horizons Away

Three horizons away,
the sea is no longer blue.
The cement sky dumps granite mountains of rain
into waves that would pulverize the Ark,
would make flying rice of the Manhattan skyline.
It rises and falls like Norse Gods
shaking out their bedsheets

Out there, it is always thirty kinds of cold,
the cold of a thousand arrows,
cold that shoots through flesh
like an x-ray through a child's lie
and cannot be described by those who haven't
felt the floor collapse from beneath their very souls.

They say, with no man 'round to hear them,
trees may never fall,
but, the ocean needs no man around
for it to conquer all.

www.ingramcontent.com/pod-product-compliance
Lightning Source LLC
Chambersburg PA
CBHW071830020426
42331CB00007B/1677